A GALAXY OF SELF-COMPOSED VERSES

SANJIT PAL

To the sacred memory of —

1. Late Kalipada Pal (My beloved grandfather)

2. Late Chapala Pal (My beloved grandmother)

3. Late Tushta Ranjan Pal (My beloved maternal grand father)

4. Late Kanaklata Pal (My beloved maternal grand mother)

5. Late Mukunda Pal (My beloved maternal uncle)

6. Late Shankar Prasad Sarkar (My beloved father-in-law)

Contents

Contents

Contents

Preface

I'm elated to know that Sanjit Pal; my Student is going to bring forth his 1st ever virgin Printed Book comprising of his self – composed Poems. A Teacher always brags about such an endeavour of his Student and I'm not an exception. I hope that each and every words of his verse will speak for his Emotion, Imagination and his Talent, also. May the Poetry of Sanjit quench the thirst of the Poetry– Lovers. I'll be eagerly waiting for his 2nd Book of Poems after a successful and wide Circulation of this present one.

Dr.Arup Kumar Ghosh

Headmaster

Kanchrapara High School (H.S.)

Kanchrapara, North 24 Parganas,

West Bengal

1. The Saviour

How strange this world is !
Many nations are hankering after
the narrow interest for ever.
No disparity, no envy
Let us stay healthy —
Should be the firm belief with clarity.
Without pondering over —
Victory or defeat.
Let us move forward to —
humanitarian target i.e.
full of feat.
Only self-centred thought —
should not be sought.
To live and lead well is our right.
Discussions should be the means
of panacea not to fight.
Ukraine-Russia war is going on —
for long.
Can't we cease it —
for the sake of peace ?
The hour of need is international peace
Let the Almighty bring amity
being the saviour of tranquility
Can we tolerate so much misery ?

Infants suffer —
From malnutrition and hunger
Lord, give away mirth
among the people's heart
Lord, shower love on the people
of this earth.
Let us stop enmity
As if, we can listen to the
Chirpings of the birds in the
Unpolluted sky with gaity.

2. Greet the New Morn

Now it is dawn.

Greeting the new morn –

Cultivators set out to reap the corn

Somewhere cries a new born

Nature attires to be calm.

With the arrival of Autumn

It is the time –

to gaze at the bright sunray

as it is the beginning of the day.

A stray dog is asleep on a log

covering the senario with dense fog.

There is stillness in the leafy wood.

Delightful is my mood.

The birds have started to coo

The boats are ready to go, too.

Listen to the cheerful voice of the bird.

That will not cease

It will continue like the rushing breeze

To soothe ambience musically

To greet the new morn gladly

When in glee grasses sway,

There is no cause of dismay.

3. The Dexterous Artist

With the advent of winter
The ambience seems to be cooler
The sun shines less brightly,
The foggy sky comes naturally.
Oranges are there to taste
Their quality appears to be best
The poor take refuge in cosy shelter
To keep them better –
To dwell in a happy corner –
In the warm nest –
Birds take rest.
Like a sunflower blooms in a bower
It is taken care of by a gardener
The dull nature disheartens us
The trees focus
Shedding their leaves
In a far land a lass lives.
Her beauty is wonderful
She is trembling in biting cold
For her, that may be harmful
The artist is dexterous for her mould.
She is a maiden of chastity
Always owns her sanctity.

4. Sweet Infancy

Who are sitting in the bowers ?
Children – as lovely as flowers
They are purely innocent
From their grandparent
They love to listen to fairy tales
They wish to roam about in the vales
They prefer to eat icecream
Sweet infancy is their cherished dream
They are the future of tomorrow
Gone is their sorrow
Everybody wants their association
Their smiles charm all with satisfaction
All wish to have a baby
Like a tiny tabby
The taste of delicious candy
Makes them extremely happy.
Hearing home-sickness for childhood
Eventually, we lose innocence in adulthood.

5. My Hollowed Love

You are my host.
Do you like me the most ?
You are in my wintry day.
You are in the spring day.
Whether bitting cold or scorching heat
You are eager to meet.
The weather is dreary –
We are weary.
But you always love me the most.
Oh! my lady-love, my host
Of you, I am boast
A fine word does not cost
You are my damzel of dream
You are like pure milk's cream
As I like thee,
I adore thee.
You are hollowed love
You are white like the dove
You admire my prosperity
You don't leave me in my adversity.

6. In the Pursuit of Excellence

We often talk about a discourse on life.
We always strife and strife
We are so reckless
We are in the pursuit of excellence
We hanker after good company
We try to shun evil company
Love is not a fantasy
Love has warmth and intimacy
It is based on dependency.
As we seek perfection,
We share our passion
If we have a robust tenacity
If we remove timidity
If we remove boredom
We'll get a hope of winning freedom
Cultivate a good habit
All hindrances you'll defeat.

7. Serene Love

I see with full of wonder.
A lass is standing, over there.
It is her dwelling —
Where she is basking
She is basking in the sun
It is her were fun
She plays with innocence
Her simplicity is essence.
She is gaining experience
Her serene love deserves reference.
She reads with dignity.
She takes care of humanity.
Her pure love has no futulity
She has no passivity
She has not negativity.
She stands for sanctity
She maintains her virginity.
Truly she is a girl of beauty.

8. Live in Harmony

Don't look down upon the poor.
They can't rejoice any more.
Don't play the game of stupidity
Approach the game of humanity
Help the needy
Worship the natural beauty
Breathe the cool breeze
But don't sneeze.
Don't involve in sin
There is purity within
Don't impure the sanctity
Always value punctuality
Always have honesty
Always have gaity
Don't try to exaggerate
Try to be everyone mate
Don't despise the destitue
Don't remain mute
In respect of despair and
Attempt hard to be a good listener
Gaze at the blue sky
Gaze at the hills high
Live and let live in harmony
Try to ignore parsimony.

9. At the Altar of Ambitions

We all should have an aim.
The target fulfilled by us is the game.
Without ambition, valueless is our emotion
It is our passion
That leads us to be famous.
None wants to be notorious.
To the cause of personal gain
We ought to have an aim.
Sacrifice at the altar of ambition
Break all sorts of inhibition
Try to reach at the top.
To get a name, hop and hop.
In life face the adversity –
Do something for the futurity
Free yourself.
Awaken yourself.
Success must usher in –
We must dwell in a happy inn
Something good will thrive
Look for that bee hive.

10. A Swing of Ecstasy

You are dear like my old garments.
I'll bear with your all torments.
Please don't be scary.
You are my star of legacy.
Let us try our dream to carry on
As you're my bassom companion,
I realize your romantic potentiality.
I wish you a bright futurity.
I want to spend time
Oh! my partner.
Warding off hindrance
You are my hidden power
If you are with me
Do I need anyone else?
Spend quality time with me
To have you I am fortunate enough
Please stand by me all through
Putting aside bitterness, if any
With me stay happy.
Enjoy every moment forgetting my offence.
You're my best defence.
Let time march on silently.
Memories will stay really.
Let there be a swing of ecstasy.

Let thy heart leap like blossoms in fantasy.

11. Astonishment

From astonishment to astonishment
I am allured to enjoyment.
I seek your sweet company.
As the bees dwell to make honey,
I crave for the warmth.
I crave for humour and mirth
Blowing the conches –
Like the horses' harness
I am in prowess,
Staying healthy by your bless.
Like the moonsoon shower,
Let us fall in the flowery bower.
To relish the euphoria –
Fulfil the desires avoiding phobia.

12. The Celestial Identity

To look at the glittering stars
To that zenith, my mind disappears.
From the distant horizon –
I want to know the unknown.
It is a huge night –
Looking beyond I see a faint light.
My heart prances in delight.
As dreams emerge that might,
To connect the celestial identity –
I am amazed at the universal enormity.
But I come to learn through intelligence,
Our life represents its transience.
Being astonished at our existence,
My intuiation pricks at conscience
In a mood of despair
Only think when dawn will appear.

13. At the Dead of Night

At the dead of night I am alone
In sleepless, in loneliness
In the quiet ambience.
I meet you in a dream
Oh, my lady-love
In the lust of vernal desire
To hope for pleasure
All hanker after.
Like blossoms bloom in the orchard
Like heart leaps in joy
In such a solitary surrounding
Caring will establish a bonding
Let dream of light hop in
I'll eradicate the darkness
Forgetting coyness.
Nurture creativity in glee.
Drop love in the sky of core
I'll drop a picture in the country
of folk-tale
I'll keep you in thirsty breast without fail.

14. Ring Out the Clarion

After a lot of waiting
Came that golden moment of meeting.
It was a stormy night.
The moonlight was not bright.
We set out for a tour.
We were both poor.
Starting the journey
Avoiding the smoky chimney
To remove the obscurity
A love-lorn longs for tense free duty
Let us touch the horizon
So as to ringout the clarion
The ripples were bobbing there.
The lovers were not for from here.
We will not cheat
Hear our hearts' beat
Maintaining secrecy we eloped with grandeur
In quest of love, our effort lasts further.

15. At Their Own Will

At their own will
Babies give out a cry that is shrill
They have a sleep soundly
Gasping and sucking done shillfully
Their capital is mother's affection
They have no evil intention
Their journey is ahead
They'll grow up leaving cosy bed
The babies who are small
Want to get a fabulous doll
This smile amuses us
This fact none will fuss
Innocence is their specimen
Teeth are as the white mountain.
Such infants run at their will
Smile will never make us chill.

16. The Worth of Existence

Our age can't be determined
Our life is predestined
Our life may have immortality
By dint of diverse creativity
Despite life's brevity.
Let us not lament over transience
If we are in good ambience,
If we are in tolerant mood,
As the gentle breezes soothe,
We take refuge in leafy wood.
Have a beautiful smile in faces.
Let us not be dejected,
Let us not be envied.
Spreading the light of optimissism
We'll forget the dim pessimism
The worth of existence none can deny
Spend time in glee
Enjoy the exuberance of joy, if any
Thinking of short span we can't flee.

17. In the Game of Dice

Most of us run after the infinite race
As if, we are in the game of dice.
Sometimes we don't think it as a malice
To earn more and more money – an addiction
Its effect is nothing but ramification
A man needs money for medication
He may have a car and house in possession.
And sufficient income to run family in ease
To the cause of trips – another expense
Thus they can do
Does he require anything else ?
We should not subdo
Money has no culmination.
We may have delusion
Like gambling too much greed
Adds to corruption
We should not infiltrate any moral degradation
Acquire asset as per needful proportion
In a joyful way, let us run a race
That'll delight us without any menace.

18. Bharat Stands United

It is the necessity of solidarity
that binds our entire country
so as to foster fraternity
among the common masses.
To live in peace and tranquility.
None can split this solidarity
This is fixed like our integal
Part of the universe and its enormity
It strengthens our harmony and unity
As we have trust in the international community
To dwell together
To think together
To flourish together
They are like our own brother
Thus, to establish universal amity
We'll try to excel in our capability
Bharat Stands united without any perplexity
Finally, the world will benefit a lot
Our good deeds will not be forgot.
Vasudhaiva Kutumbakam's is our vision
We must not deviate ourselves from that mission.

19. A Damsel

She – a damsel of graceful physique
To hug her is unique
Standing under an Oak
She wears a beautiful clock
A girl of promise
A lass of heavenly bliss
She herself is an edifice
Fitted with chemise
I am not to flatter
The damsel is a heart breaker
All day long
For her I long
To dine with her
To ride with her
To swim in a river
She is my heart's listener
She is always in my vision
She stands by me in every situation.

20. Let the Passion Be Brighter

Let my soul take on a lovely journey
Only I'll listen to your nostalgic melody
Your time is really timeless
That is not charmless
That echoes delight and harmony
Your song will never be forgotten
Let the passing brighter
Feeling us to highten
Your music will entertain
It is a source of pleasure
It will remain as a vast treasure
Let love shower
I want to encounter
Your music seems to be cursory
I am unaware of that glory
You are full of vitality
That gives me aesthetic sensibility

21. With the Passage of Time

With the passage of time
The change will be fine
Being a worshipper of nature
We must not torture our nature
Then she will revenge in future
A man spends from his infancy
To the old age of dependency.
By gone days will never come.
We've to be tolerant and calm
We may indulge with fancy
But we should not invite despudency.
Frustration may come in one's life
To tackle it we must strife
If we can avert worry
Our life will be full of merry.
Our all aspirations may not be speedy
A wave of panic is not the remedy.
We should be enthralled by the beauty.
We've to save our habitat with gaity.
We've to adore one's ability.
My verse does not glorify war but its pity.
To the cause of civilization
Cease war which is not a solution.
I must opine

with the passage of time
Everything will be okay and fine.

• 24 •

22. Lo! The Butterfly

Oh Butterfly ! Oh butterfly !
With you I want to fly
From me don't go away.
Please do come everyday.
You feel the neetar of a flower
Spread your wings in a bower
Oh Butterfly ! I want to have your joy
Lo! the Butterfly is very coy
Like an unmarried spinster
The butterfly's shyness is an enchanter
I love your sweet beauty
I'll catch if I get an opportunity.
I want to know the cause of your glee.
With you I want to flee.
Please do come everyday.
Your company will make me gay.
I'll not listen to your excuse.
Come across me in profuse.

23. A Winner

Who wants to be a loser ?
Everyone wants to be a winner
A winner is an achiever
A winner is a gainer.
A winner is a path-finder
A winner is a successful builder
A winner must have an ethical character
He will lead for ever
He who wins is a great thinker
A winner maintains a good follower
Winners act in a unique way
Their footprints shall be today.
A person nurtures his patentiality
A person who fulfils his credibiltiy
Gets the warmth of gaity
A winner creates a thing of beauty
Thus, a winner enjoys honour
To win must be the hunger.

24. Our Journey By Boat

A boat journey starts on Sunday morning
At that time ripples were rolling
Aimlessly we were moving
Merrily little birds were singing
In the Ganges we were swimming
In the bright sun waves were dancing
Lovely flowers were tossing
Forgetting enmity
We were in an aura of amity.
Nature charmed us with beauty
Beside the river, it is full of guity
Various families came home
They were involved in game.
The time we have passed is cheerful
The sight was really beautiful.
In a word, it was wonderful.
It was the time of summar vacation.
As if, it was a great occasion.
The air is filled with smell
We've forgotten the pangs of hell.
God, give us valour
So that we might be the conqueror.

None will chide
Nothing to hide.
On the bank the fishermen were there
We've came to have pleasure here
Though the weather was hot
The gentle breeze welcomed our boat.
The crimson rays of the setting sun
It is a matter of great fun.
I wanted to share something
We came back home in the evening.

25. Tagore! You Should be Living at this Junction

Tagore! You should be living at this juncture
We're being disturbed by external torture.
We're not moved by the charms of Nature.
Money is the meditation of our present and future.
In our mind there is no peace.
The lover has no boldness to kiss
Now, we've forgotten him.
Frustration is our only hymn.
With us love is no more –
With it, faithless is our core.
Motherland is passing through a critical condition,
Everywhere is found political corruption.
There is not a place for rest ;
It seems, death is the best.
Time is fleeting away fast
Undone works are found vast.
To read Tagore there is no mood,
So ignorance is our only food.
True joy is found to be rare.
Having no happiness, heart is bare.

26. Folly

Most of us become victim of folly
Sometimes it comes naturally
Sometimes it comes unawarely
Being puzzled, we behave oddly
Some make it jolly
Some accuse blatantly
Think for a while
Take it as a gile
Relish the plausible moment
Avert embarrassing comment
There is nothing for a hue and cry
At a little distance we can try
Circumstances will change suddenly
Will anything occur unluckily ?
Patience is like a treasure
Providing us limitless pleasure –
All will trust finally
Folly is subject to teach something really.
Make the situation fit
Keep us in a cordial spirit.

27. The Time to Kiss

Oh, my beloved reader

I want to be a writer

Please allow me some space.

Look at your face.

Please don't hiss

It is the time to kiss

Oh, my lady-love

I want to have your love.

The roses must bloom every year

Don't get fear

Oh, dear !

Shed no tear

Oh, dear

I adore thee.

I love thee.

Please don't miss

It is the time to kiss.

28. The Tapestry of Fine Moments

I would prefer to say.
With you I want to stay.
My life becomes charming falling in love.
Purest form of love –
Comes from the depth of core
Thoughts go on to share funny talks
True emotions hit the heart like the tales of lore.
Spreading lots of happiness
Oh, my princess
Listen to the loving talks
With care that will carry on
With warmth and shyness.
Let me forget the time which is lost
Let the moon shine.
Now we are at the prime time
Of vigour and youth.
Nothing makes us apart.
I just want for ever
I'll sew the tapestry of
fine moments together!
How lovely together
How lovely your looks are!

Unknowingly you come to my life
Establishing perpetual friendship
None can break that relationship.

• 33 •

29. Wipe Out the Misery

We have to ponder over
We'll try better
A gang of jobless workers
Causing slumber-breakers
They have no father to guide
They are mob to chide
They have no leading light
Among them selves they fight
Owing to lack of motivation.
Their trajeetory leads to intoxication
Everyone must have an ambition.
Some want to be a teacher
Some want to be a lawyer
Some want to be a doctor
Some want to be a contractor
Why wants to be a prisoner ?
None is born as an offender
Where to go for work ?
The place is dark
We've to be sympathetic
We've to be co-operative
We're to wipe out the miserary of them
The society can't uplift without them.

30. Will - Power

Have firm will-power
To be a winner
Have truth in yourself
Have faith in yourself
To be a gainer
Don't scared of losing
Today is the hour of healthy fighting.
Then, everything will be amazing
Strive for the great initiative
For the good be speculative
Don't split your heart's core
There's something to give more
It is the endeavour
That is like our life's grandeur
That assists us to aspire
To make positive thinking higher
If we've firm will-power
Obstacles to overcome
The best is yet to come.

31. We, the Teachers

We, the teachers
Are the pupils' future makers
We, the nation builders
We guide the job seekers
We build the students' career
We, the philosopher
We, the mentor
Are the good orator
We, the thinker
Have the life changing power
We take the responsibility
To form the students' cognitive ability
We teach to get better
We teach how to score higher
We praise the aestic creativity of the learners
We mould the learner's character
We train the taught
Pupils, forget us not
We can see the mirror
As we are preceptor
We inspire to learn more and more
Mercy is in our core
As we are in teaching profession,
Our dedication is for true education.

32. Be a Man

On this moment of grace
I want to embrace
The elegance that is timeless.
Is it full of boredom
Being alone ?
Who is the princess
Having such lovely eyes ?
Your beauty is at high prices
Let feel winter fur
With lots of love and gladness
Shun all laziness
Is it not amazing
Loneliness does not seen boring
Let dive into the speculation of credibility
Although false have surrounds
Discovering simplicity
Build a genuine personality
Be a man with a unique identity
May you shine with potentiality.

33. The Bird

Behold at the hill
There sits a bird to thrill.
Do have a glance
Though it is not a fareway place
The breeze is blowing softly.
The bird is singing sweetly.
The aroma of flowers scatter around
Beside the ditch fish abound
The bird wants to soar in glee
Whereas the timid want to flee
The bird an epitome of emotion
Does not approve subjugation.
As the bird sings liberally,
He fulfils his dreams boldly
As the bird is not abed
He is not confined
He only experiences the natural beauty
He craves for people's equality
The bird sings and sings freely
The day the bird passes is lovely.

34. In My Core

It was the Sharad Purnima night.
Everywhere were the rays of moonlight.
I was speechless to see the natural beauty.
Mind was fresh with totality.
What a splendid sight !
The sky was clear and bright.
It seems I am in paradise.
Listen to my advice.
Removing the weeds
My endeavour is for the good deeds
My lot is shining
My valour is not diminishing
I must confess
I like thy face
I crave for sound health –
That is the wealth
In the pursuit of a chance,
My heart wants to dance
My disappointment is over.
I want to keep you in my core forever.

35. Love Me For Ever

Love me for ever
Dwell with me for ever
You are my love my dear
I am your beloved lover
You embrace me.
They love will enkindle me.
You are in my core
I'll love you more and more
I like your eyes
We appreciate the blue skies.
You are in my memory
Have ambition in glory
We adore the lovely night
Almight, bring us light.
It is our fate
We are eternal mate
Always crave for laughter
We'll reside by a river.
God, eredicate our pain
To us, you are main.
We must not regret
We must not forget
We'll go together everywhere
Peaceful abode in our atmosphere

Guitar sings in the wind
That leads to equal mind.
You are my pleasure
Your love is my treasure
You are my guest
Mere lonely is our rest.
True love is our passion.
Your glamour is everlasting the fashion.

36. Aspiration

I have a tale
I want to tell
There are two options ahead
Success or failure, I said
Aspiration for the best
Do utilise your rest
We should trust our action —
As action reflects our aspiration.
If anything wrongs occur,
Whatever calamity may incur
Removing stress, face the disaster
Will permission come later ?
I say never, never
Look beyond, that is, inspiration
Your life is a trip to motivation
Then you'll find success not far
Achievement may be near.
Success never comes magically
Hope must not be abandoned whimsically.

37. Benign Presence

I long for your company as before
I want to love you more and more.
I look for you affectionately
You come to my reverie occasionally
I find pleasure in your association.
I adore thy intense passion
I need you urgently
I find you rapidly
Your benign presence enthralls me
Your attraction captivates me
I do feel morose –
When I fail to give you a rose
Truly your love is divine
It will last for a long time
I am your lover boy
For me it is a matter of joy
Take my friendship
As a lover, I am not selfish.

38. Vain Love-making

I'm the captain of my fate
I have no fear
Death is knocking at the gate
Its cruel hand will snatch, my dear
Don't shed tears for me —
Because death sets out soul free.
Look at the north pole
It is fixed for ever.
So no lamentation, my dear
Imperishable is my soul.
Our love-making has gone in vain
We must succeed in heaven.

39. A Damsel of Purity

Here is a girl
Her lock is curl
She wears pearl
She is nine
She looks fine
Her eyes are bright
She believes in might
She dislikes fright
She is a lass of beauty
She lives for futurity
She is an innocent girl.
She is a lovely girl
She is a damsel of purity
She is a damsel of sanctity
She welcomes me gracefully
She loves me dearly
From the inner core
For me she will be alive more and more
When my lady-love's song vibrates,
My heart palpitates.

40. The Rose

The rose lovely rose –
A symbol of friendship and love-dose
In my garden –
When daylight has broaden
When the roses bloom,
They remove my gloom.
When the sun rises,
The roses glitter.
Birds twitter.
When they dwindle in the air,
Fragrance catches our ear.
When I rest at home,
I look at them
The beautiful sight inspires me
And I sing in praise of them.

41. An Eligible Diplomat

To tell straight cut
Chanakya – a noted diplomat.
Being a man of wide wit
It deserved to be fit
A person of extensive thought
For us he taught and taught
He was a scholar out and out.
In it, there was no doubt.
The forerunner in the spread of intellect
As a statesman he was adept.
He remained at the pedestral of logicality.
He was endowed with creativity.
He was a man of amiable disposition.
He had a good observation.
As an eligible diplamat of principle
Such a statue really credible
He knew about his propriety
Briefly, he was a rare personality
His works will lead us to cherish
His popularity will never perish.
Even today, he is remembered in History.
Truly, a matter of glory.

42. Holi

Holi – the festival of colour

Enjoy its euphoria with laughter.

We should observe it with safety

We should celebrate it with gaity.

In our mind, we ought to be pure.

Its exuberance we must endure

Let it be celebrated pompously

Let the day of 'Holi' relish beautifully

In spring this festival comes –

Taking the plethora of grapes

Let love be bestowed

In the affinity those are endowed

'Holi' festival will come another year –

Removing the monotony and fear.

Let us make Holi delightful.

This is not the time to be mournful.

43. The Year

The year comes and goes
Memory remains in holes
Many occurrences take place
We have no way but to grace.
Life is a blending of weal and woe
We've to admit friend and foe.
Ecstasy will follow sorrow.
We should not borrow.
If we can bear with the tragedies
We'll not suffer from anxieties.
We've to pass the time in glee.
Out of fear, never try to flee.
Recollect the delightful days
Forget those mournful days.
The year comes and goes.
Amidst suffering mind rejoices.
The year must be prosperous,
If we are joyous.

44. A New Millennium

A man has to do something
Is mere longivity — the end of living ?
All men crave for fame.
All men crave for name.
Many men strive.
But the question must arise.
Atmosphere few succeed,
All crave for a noble deed
A main achievement is judged by his deed
Who has forgot ? –
Our life span is short.
Think that are beautiful –
Think us delightful.
A new millennium will usher in
The world is changing
For greater people are striving
Don't want time in mere thinking
Having no intense fear
Do something for ones who are near.
Crave for noble action
Bear the torch of a good civilization
Greatness will emerge for the next generation.

45. She Will Conquer

On a winter night
There was no might
So that she can fight
None can redress her plight
To relish she shares no right.
Having no woolen garment
She has to torment
The day was rainy
She has a lass who is tiny
She has nowhere to go
She roams to and fro
She has to tolerate the snowy day
This is her life, her way
She wants to remain hale.
But circumstances lead her to hell.
Lacking in amity
She suffers from insecurity.
She faces everything boldly
The clouds are sailing joyously
Oneday, she will conquer ultimately.
As her valour will withstand, finally.

46. In Such a Way

We have to live in such a way –
So that we may be gay
We have to be like a beautiful flower –
That blooms in a bower.
Such a flower gives us recreation
Removing our frustration.
We want such a room
Where there will be no gloom.
If we shun idleness,
Our conviction will move towards cheefulness.
We have to tackle the situation in such a way.
So that we may be gay.
Always work hard promptly,
Accept the challenge gladly
The sunrise is not far away
If we guide ourselves in a fair way.
Be amused at the taughest incident
Free joy is our only commitment
Let pass anxiety
Then healthy life is not in perplexity
We should lead a humble life
Family will last to have a good wife.

47. 'Kash' Flowers in Autumn

Who does not want a toy ?
Who does not want a feeling of joy ?
Who does not like the peacock dance ?
Who does not enjoy such at a glace ?
As we enjoy fantasy
We all hanker after ecstasy.
If you study literature,
Be a lower of nature.
'Kash' flowers beside a river
spell the nature lovers.
Kash flowers are tossing,
They are moving
They are dancing in the air.
They are really lovely and fair
Whether is low or high mood
They are my imaginary food
The 'kash' flowers bloom in Autumn in glee
From there none wants to flee.
Their span is never-ending
Truly Kash flowers are heart-throbbing.

48. A Fearless Fighter

All adore a fearless fighter
Such a man is never a deceiver
He admires his valour
As he is not a timid warrior
He is the father of bravery
Lacking in deceivery
He drinks life to the dregs
Some beg anyone's pregs
He knows how to fall in love
He knows how to nurture love
He accepts everything gladly
He loves all dearly.
His eyes are not tearful
He stands courgeous and dauntful
Oh! behold, listen to what I say
Nothing can stop you away, away
With a blade I have a sword
I am not a coward
That I am a moor
Came to my door
Have your lips a smile
Let there be light to the saddle
Here I am not vile
Please kiss me and smile.

49. Rain

No scorching heat again
After the heat comes the rain
From studies students abstain
No afraid of Exam-pain
Rain, Rain, Come Again
Blossoms will bloom
We have no gloom
Trees have become green.
Our environment has been clear
We always hanker after shower
We have no anxiety or fear
In studies the taught pay attention
For your better comprehension
People are taking shelter
To take refuge in a tree near
Now we are devoid of temperature
There is no heat of torture
I am fond of rain
So I hail refreshing rain
Birds feel appetite for food
I am in joyful mood,
I don't run after fame.
I welcome rain.
Now the peasants will gain.

Rain is not uncommon
It is a natural phenomenon
Though rain is not too much,
It has given us a healing touch.

50. A Didactic Lesson

The birds' music is sweet to hear
The birds' music is sweet to bear
A lass is singing nearby
Oh, passers-by
Let her sing
Let her bring
That will remove our sorrow
Never try to borrow
We eat to live
Bees are in a hive
To walk is good for health
Good health is our wealth
Help the needy
Don't be greedy
Assist the poor
Get the joy more and more.
Don't hanker after money
It cannot be our only honey
Steal never
It is a sin for eyes
Don't play in foul weather
Try to live together
It is a cold winter night.
Against it although fight.

God will bring boom
We'll not go towards doom.

51. The poor

The winter is near.
The poor are in fear
They suffer the most
Their luck is the worst
They are jobless
They are homeless
They have no follower
They have no shelter
They are the victim of mockery
They are the victim of trickery
They can't play gaily
They can't mix freely
The prices are on the rise
They are facing demise.
The poor are confused.
The poor are refused.
As there is no charity,
They roam in the city
Aimlessly, hopelessly
Though they lead honestly
The poor believe firmly
They work silently.

52. Honesty

Honesty is the best policy.
A noble virtue is merey.
Be a great man.
Be a good human.
You are a boy.
You are not coy.
Eat a lot of water
Eat a little sugar
Breathe pure air
Eat in a pot of copper
What I like —
You must take pride
In what you think and abide
In the east sunrises.
In the tree bird lives
At night shines the moon
You'll be healthy soon.
Have power
Have valour
Now you are a pupil
Try to avoid evil.
Eat milk
Don't wear silk
You you're a blooming flower

Try to lift up to the tower.
Buid your good personality.
Honesty is the best policy.
Never too hot nor cold.
You must be bold.
Practise Yoga well.
Peacefully you can dwell
Knowledge is your treasure.
It'll add to your pleasure.
You yourself try to measure –
For the sake of inner pleasure,
Target your aim
Profit will add to gain.

53. The Spring

The cooings of the cuckoo recall —
The spring is about to fall.
The unseen bird ! Carry on your singing
My inner core is beating.
The full noon is about to rise at night.
The natural scenario is beautiful and bright
I am ready to welcome the spring
No doubt, it will bring
Endless love and delight for us.
The spring abandance of fruits — an ecstasy for us.
From bushes to bushes
We cann't avoid the flowers' fragrance
In mood we feel great joyance
Palash, Simul, Krishnachura are laughing
The pleasure weather makes us charming.
The spring is not too hot
It is not too cold, infact
As the spring has come to our door,
There is no hour to lament any more.

54. Celebrating a Day

Her eyes are bright.
Her eyes shine at night.
The hills are vast.
Learn from the past.
I am elated at her beauty.
I am elated at her purity.
I am exited.
I am captivated.
I am delighted.
She has submitted.
The sea is roaring.
The ripples are rolling.
She is merrily singing.
She likes to play with clay
It is a matter of happy day
The girl and I am joyful
The girl and I am cheerful
Our gladness knows no bounds
Our happiness knows no bounds
We want to cheer up.
We want to warm up.
Our togetherness passed many a day
It demands us celebrating a day.

55. To Err is Human

The sun has set.
The beauty of its beams I cann't forget.
The gentle breeze is blowing
Our Nature is calling
All the trees are shedding their leaves.
The Bees are in the hive.
Our destination is long
I can listen to the song –
Which the birds are chirping.
A new shirt a tall man is wearing.
I can't ignore the path.
There is a unique thing, but
The might is coming
The pupils are preparing
The lessons that is homework –
They never forget their work.
Shun your gun.
Because to err is human
The sun has set.
Now it's time to bed.
What a fine sight !
It looks bright even at night.
I have a lot of money
I intend to set out a journey.

56. The Fate of Nation

Think of our country.
Think of her security.
Maintain road safety.
Shoulder a great responsibility.
Do noble deed
You'll be immortal, indeed
Follow the path of Greatman.
Be a good human.
For good, always strive
It'll be a matter of pride
Love the bovine animal
Be social
Hanker after the highest position
Don't choose contradiction
Love demoracy
Fight for supremacy
Fight against foreign invasion
Bear the torch of civilization
Think deeply
Remove anxiety perpetually
Live in peace.
It is the bliss.
That will lead to a carefree life
Then you will not deprive

Try to enhance the fate of nation
Take the correct decision.
Judge pragmatically
Then all things will seem brightly.

57. The Key to Greatness

It is the reality —
We have infinite capability
It is the industry —
That leads to success in nobility
If you think sagaciously
If you act sincerely,
If you have determination,
That leads to a good action.
If you do spend time idly,
Achievement must not come surely.
Hard toil is a necessity.
Hail universal fraternity.
For the the globe bring progress.
This is the key to greatness.
Please be hard-working
Make life worth-living.

58. The Leader

Everyone seems to be a leader
He may be a doctor
He may be a warrior
He may be a teacher
He may be a barrister
He may be a writer
A leader must be an orator
A leader must have a sense of humour
A leader is a managing director
A person who is a good leader –
Must be always a winner.
Leadership forms one's career
Leadership guides a motivation speaker.
Everyone wants to be a leader.
He may be a joker or a politician
He may be a composer or a magician
Whether a diplomat or a statesman
Leadership leads to be a greatman
A key to success is leadership
Such as relations build friendship
To be a good leader
We've to be a good listener
To face the challenge, build a good quality
People will remember a leader with nobility.

59. The Sea

I want to go on a journey.
The day will be windy.
I will listen to the song.
My voyage will be long.
It is the time of morning.
The sails are trembling.
The sea is calling me.
The bright star is calling me.
The star will guide me.
The voyage will delight me.
I anticipate the indomitable call
My aspiration will be perpetual
The seascape is lovely.
Ripples are making joyfully
Fog is in the haze
Beyond ashore cows graze
I seek no company.
Undisturbed nap is my company.

60. A Step Back

To take a step back
And to embrace the nostalgia
Of my boyhood and I am taken aback
Gone are the days of enjoyment that fill
I can proud to feel
The memories still remain treasured
I cherish those to be deserved.
To be noted, not be forgotten
Not to be hidden.
Those astonishing experience
That captivate me
That help me to cherish
That help me to forget bitter anguish
In the pursuit of those cheerful
Ward off all worries
To render me joyance
Dreams that come true add to
Contentment for the future days with excellence
To promote my creativity with brilliance.

61. Lead a carefree life

We crave for a dwelling place
Happy dwelling gives us solace.
You'll find
Worries haunt the mind
Remove your anxieties
Anxieties lead to tragedies
Learn to tolerate suffering
Stop the notion of attacking.
Fulfill your mission
Your life is your vision.
Shun your evil habits totally.
Life will be blissful perpetually
We'll love glorious
We'll love glamour.
We've to suffer
Lead a carefree life.
It is better to strive
Bad activites bring doom
Happiness will go to your room.
Happiness will go to your room.
If there is corruption
There will be more degradation
Success in life brings prossperity,
Foster universal fraternity

You avoid dishonesty.
You must have infinite capacity
Have patience.
You'll find joyance.

62. Keep Quiet

Keep silent
Don't be violent
No fear,
No anger,
Have courage.
Have knowledge
Face the situation boldly.
Face the silence carefully,
Do the work firmly
Do the work swiftly
Don't run in the sun
Lough and make fun.
Have faith in God.
You be glad.
Be cheerful.
Be careful.
Don't be agressive.
Try to be comprehensive.
Keep quiet
Have balanced diet
This shoud be the go of today
You'll be happy oneday.

63. A Citizen of a Society

We should have an accountability
As we are a citizen of a society.
We should encourage charity.
We must discourage disparity.
We'll live in a good book
Futuristic good is our outlook.
We'll seek cosiness and happiness
But we ought to treat all with kindness.
There must be basic needs.
We'll not forget our benevolent deeds.
We'll face woes on the way
But remember, weal will come oneday.

64. Time and Tide

Time and Tide no wait for man
It is known to all man and woman
No one can keep hold of time
No one can stop the speed of stream.
One moment of time is very important ;
But the rapid flow of rivulet is less significant.
While Time is gone,
It is for ever gone.
Tide flows silently ;
It leaves a good result surely.
Tide mixes with the vast ocean.
But time mixes with the eternal heaven.

65. Live for Today

Dead is the past
So past is past
We'll live for today
Don't worry over next day
Don't think too much about future
Bad thinking brings mental torture
Don't really the incident of the part
Because lifetime is not vast.
So I must say –
Earthly objects must decay
Only true love can stay
Till the doom's day.

66. A Bright Future Ahead

Can we afford
All that we want
By the use of sword ?
Certainly we won't
By the use of muscle.
Will the people be in tussle ?
The sword may instigate animosity.
As it can't bring tranquility,
This is mere transitory.
Good thought will last till glory.
Avoiding hatred and anger
Establish true love for ever.
The sword can win our body.
Muscle power is not liked by everybody.
So do good for the people –
That will be indeed, gainful.
If we can conquer hatred,
Surely a bright future ahead.

67. Chandrayaan-3 Lands on the Moon

A great news for the global fraternity
Finally, Chandrayaan-3 is successful
After a long tenacity.
Being an Indian, I am boastful
Our mission comes true.
To the TV, our eyes remain glue.
Chandrayaan-3 lands on the moon.
It is a gift of scientific boon.
Our technology has crossed the infinite.
Criticism is there, despite
Its glory none can ignore.
For ever, it will last in our core.
Generation after generation
We know the cosmos through intuition.
The lines of my verse will uphold—
The fact that we can, as we are bold.
Our pride is not for the negativity.
We will attempt to foster creativity.
We will shine and sing for humanity
Forgetting our life's brevity.